Laura Purdie Salas

Illustrated by
Micha Archer

Snowman – Cold = Puddle

Spring Equations

Charlesbridge

As winter gray drains away, spring tiptoes in. It sprinkles color and motion and sound all around. Each sunny day, soft breeze, and spring shower changes our world.

science + poetry = surprise!

Science is why and how a flower grows. Poetry is looking at that flower and seeing a firework. Surprise!

EARLY SPRING

warmth + light = alarm clock

During the winter, some animals hibernate to survive the cold. As they snooze, their heart rate and breathing s l o w   w a y   d o w n. Hibernating animals wake up when spring days grow warmer and longer.

snowman − cold = puddle

Water is a shape-shifter.
In northern winters, it
might fall as snow. But
when spring temperatures
rise above freezing, snow
melts into water. Sad news
for snowmen!

As mountaintop snows melt in spring, the water flows downhill and joins rivers rolling toward the ocean. A stream can swell into a racing river, just for spring!

stream + snowmelt = stampede!

riverbank + otters = playground

Some animals play all year long. In spring, otters slip and slide in the dirty, slushy snow. No mittens. No hats. Just messy, muddy, mucky fun.

bark + beak = drum

Tap. Tap. Tap. A downy woodpecker digs for bugs in a tree. *Tap-tap-tap-tap-tap-tap-tap!* It drums faster in spring to claim its territory or attract a mate.

maple trees x buckets + boiling = sticky smile

Maple syrup starts with trees. When spring days warm up but nights still freeze, sugary sap flows beneath maple trees' bark. People collect the sap and boil it down until it is thick and sticky and perfect for pancakes.

BIG beaver + BIG beaver = little beaver

Happy birthday! Many baby animals are born in spring. A newborn beaver kit weighs less than a loaf of bread. A spring birthday gives it plenty of time to grow and learn survival skills before winter comes.

talons + pond = fast food

In spring, bald eagles that wintered down south fly north again. On their way to the northern United States and Canada, they swoop down to scoop up tasty fish dinners.

sky + goose

+ goose

+ goose

+ goose

+ goose

+ goose

+ goose = arrow

Each spring, many geese migrate north to gobble up tender, tasty new grasses. Geese fly in a *V* for speed. The front birds' air currents help carry the back birds. They all take turns in front and back.

bushes x blooms = perfume

Lilac blooms are spring's perfume. The sweet scent invites insects and birds to visit. These important visitors track pollen from flower to flower, like tracking mud from room to room. Humans just enjoy the wonderful smells.

breeze + kite = ballet

In spring, the sun sails higher in the sky. It shines down and warms the air near the ground. As the warm air rises, wind rushes in to fill the empty space. That creates billowy, blustery kite-flying days!

bumblebees x flowers = blueberries

Bees help feed us! When bees sip nectar from spring flowers, they help spread pollen from one plant to another. Plants need this pollination to grow juicy blueberries and other fruits.

nest + robin = jewelry box

Robins lay dazzling blue eggs in spring. Some scientists believe that the most vivid blue eggs have the healthiest chicks inside. The blue shells might act like sunscreen, protecting the chicks from sun damage before they hatch.

hive + bees − bees + bees = airport

In spring, scout honeybees leave their hive to find food. When they succeed, they return to spread the word. Bees fly out. In. Out. In. Out. In. You could get dizzy watching busy bees!

lake + warmth = sky castles

In many places, spring is the wettest season. Rain is part of the earth's never-ending water cycle. Water falls, flows into lakes and rivers and to the sea, evaporates, and forms clouds. Then the cycle begins all over again.

deer + tree = umbrella

What do animals do when it rains? Deer might huddle beneath branches, using a tree as a big leafy umbrella.

seeds − umbrella = flowers

Have you heard the saying "April showers bring May flowers"? Animals might hide from spring rain, but plants drink it up! Seeds need soil, air, and plenty of water to grow.

sun − storm = rainbow

Rainbows also need rain. (It's right there in their name!) A rainbow appears when it's sunny where you are, but raining nearby. Raindrops bend sunlight, so it separates into different colors. Rainy spring days are perfect for rainbow spotting.

LATE SPRING

dusk + skunks = parade

Late spring means feeding lessons for baby skunks. Skunks are nocturnal, so as day turns to evening, a mama skunk marches through the meadow to look for grubs and bugs for supper. Her kits follow her, watching and learning.

1 dandelion x 1 breath = 100 parachutes

Dandelions are a weedy, seedy sign of spring. Plants spread their seeds in many ways. Dandelion seeds float on the wind—or your breath. One seed might drift five hundred miles before landing!

frogs + night = symphony

In the spring, male frogs croon their hearts out to an audience of female frogs. Different species have unique voices, like the different instruments of an orchestra. Gray treefrogs chirp high and fast like piccolos. Bullfrogs honk low and loud on their watery trombones.

On clear, dark nights, constellations shimmer across the sky. In spring, the water serpent Hydra slithers overhead and Leo the lion stalks the night. The hero Hercules raises his club, ready to take on both creatures.

sky − day = stories

you + the world = ?

Spring changes the world,
and it might change you, too.
What happens when you
explore the wonders of
spring? That's an equation
only *you* can solve!

Author's Note

"Within poetry and science beat the twin hearts of observation and imagination."

—Heidi Mordhorst, poet and teacher

I am in awe of the scientific processes that make sunsets, storms, and, of course, spring. But when I look at our amazing world, I don't see just science. I also see stories and pictures. A snowman melts overnight, and I see heat as a thief, stealing snowpeople and sledding hills. Deer huddle under a dripping maple tree, and I see kids sharing a spring-green umbrella. Dandelion fluff scatters, and I see hundreds of skydivers opening tiny parachutes.

Scientists and poets search the world and find knowledge and wonder in equal parts. The equations in this book explore the reasons for the changes we see in spring. These combinations of words and symbols are science. But they are also something more. They compress big ideas into small phrases, using unexpected or playful language. And they ask you to look at common things in new ways. They are poetry.

In writing these equation poems, I began to notice things that I usually take for granted. I hope you notice how our world changes every day all around us. You don't have to live anywhere in particular or use special equipment to appreciate how the world transforms in spring.

You just have to notice.

—Laura Purdie Salas

Illustrator's Note

Reading the words of a new story for the first time is like unwrapping a present. Each sentence fills me with a rush of possible ways to make the words come alive. I doodle ideas in the manuscript's margins and then fill sketchbook after sketchbook. Things I don't know enough about I research. When I am happy with each scene, I make a tiny version of the book called a dummy. It's tiny because I have learned that if a composition reads clearly small, then it will usually work large, too.

For this book I thought back to winters and springs in my own life. Spring in New England meant we could finally ride our bikes again, take off our jackets, catch tadpoles at the pond in bare feet in the cold mud, and play in our fort under the bright yellow flowering forsythia bush.

Spring = color for me, and I love color! This book is illustrated using collage. To prepare my papers, I layered tissue paper, did crayon-rubbing resist with watercolor washes, used my homemade stamps, and spread acrylic paint thinly over colored papers with a credit card. Then I cut, sliced, snipped, punched, ripped, trimmed, clipped, and glued down the papers, leaving the children's faces to be done in oil paints.

—Micha Archer

When Spring Starts

Maybe you are waiting for spring. You're excited for kites and puddles and ducklings and baseball games. But when does spring actually begin?

That's a hard question to answer. Where you live affects when you will experience spring. For instance, in late March, Minnesota kids might still be building snowmen, while Florida kids are splashing in the Atlantic Ocean. Here are a few different definitions of when spring begins.

- Meteorologists (scientists who study weather): after the end of the three coldest months in any specific place
- Astronomers (scientists who study space): on the spring equinox, when day and night are the same length (between March 19 and 21 for the northern hemisphere)
- Gardeners: when the last wintry frost is thawing, daffodils are blooming, and seeds are whispering, "Sow me. Water me."
- Kids in northern climates: when grown-ups don't force you to wear a heavy coat anymore

Further Reading

Spring
Abracadabra, It's Spring! by Anne Sibley O'Brien (rhyming nonfiction)

Everything Spring by Jill Esbaum (nonfiction)

When Spring Comes by Kevin Henkes (nonfiction)

Weather
Blue on Blue by Dianne White (rhyming fiction)

Rainbow by Marion Dane Bauer (nonfiction)

When the Wind Blows by Linda Booth Sweeney (rhyming fiction)

Growing Things
And Then It's Spring by Julie Fogliano (fiction)

Seed to Plant by Kristin Baird Rattini (nonfiction)

Spring Blossoms by Carole Gerber (rhyming nonfiction)

Water
All the Water in the World by George Ella Lyon (poetic nonfiction)

Water Can Be . . . by Laura Purdie Salas (rhyming nonfiction)

Bees
Flight of the Honey Bee by Raymond Huber (nonfiction)

Maple Syrup
From Maple Tree to Syrup by Melanie Mitchell (nonfiction)

Birds
Mama Built a Little Nest by Jennifer Ward (rhyming nonfiction)

A Nest Is Noisy by Dianna Hutts Aston (nonfiction)

Constellations
Constellations by F. S. Kim (nonfiction)

At the time of publication, all URLs printed in this book were accurate and active. Charlesbridge,
the author, and the illustrator are not responsible for the content or accessibility of any website.

Published by Charlesbridge
9 Galen Street
Watertown, MA 02472
(617) 926-0329
www.charlesbridge.com

Library of Congress Cataloging-in-Publication Data
Names: Salas, Laura Purdie, author. | Archer, Micha, illustrator.
Title: Snowman − cold = puddle: spring equations/Laura Purdie Salas; illustrated by Micha Archer.
Other titles: Snowman minus cold equals puddle | Spring equations
Description: Watertown, MA: Charlesbridge, [2019]
Identifiers: LCCN 2017056287 | ISBN 9781580897983 (reinforced for library use)
 | ISBN 9781632896445 (ebook pdf) | ISBN 9781632896438 (ebook)
Subjects: LCSH: Spring—Juvenile literature. | Seasons—Juvenile literature.
Classification: LCC QB637.5 .S25 2019 | DDC 508.2—dc23
 LC record available at https://lccn.loc.gov/2017056287

Printed in China
(hc) 10 9 8 7 6 5 4 3 2

Illustrations done in oils and custom-made collage papers on gessoed paper
 then manipulated in Photoshop
Display type set in Graphen by Maciej Wloczewski
Text type set in Museo by Jos Buivenga/exljbris
Color separations by Colourscan Print Co Pte Ltd, Singapore
Printed by 1010 Printing International Limited in Huizhou, Guangdong, China
Production supervision by Brian G. Walker
Designed by Martha MacLeod Sikkema